hissssss

meh-eh-eh

clomp

clomp

woof!

cluck

clap

woof!

cluck

clap

meow

bang

bang

quack

quack

neigh neigh

baa-baa

oink

baa-baa

oink

tra-la-la

baa-baa

baa-baa

Wake up

hee haw

baa-baa

baa-baa

Library of Congress Cataloging-in-Publication Data
Thomson, Ruth
All About Sounds.

(My first easy and fun books)
Bibliography: p.
Summary: Jim and all the farm animals make sounds trying to wake up the cow sleeping in the middle of the road.
[1. Sound--Fiction. 2. Animal sounds--Fiction] I. Rees, Mary, ill. II. Title. III. Series: Thomson, Ruth. My first easy and fun books.
PZ7.T38So 1987   [E]   87-42589
ISBN 1-55532-338-3
ISBN 1-55532-313-8 (lib. bdg.)

North American edition first published in 1987 by
Gareth Stevens, Inc.
7221 West Green Tree Road Milwaukee, WI 53223, USA

First published as *Sounds* in the United Kingdom by Walker Books Ltd.

Typeset by Web Tech, Inc., Milwaukee. Printed in Italy.
Series Editor: MaryLee Knowlton.

1 2 3 4 5 6 7 8 9 92 91 90 89 88 87

MY FIRST EASY AND FUN BOOKS

ALL ABOUT

sounds

By Ruth Thomson
Illustrated by Mary Rees

Gareth Stevens Publishing
Milwaukee

Jim and his children were
taking their vegetables to town.

But there was Daisy, fast
asleep in the middle of the road.

Jim **shouted.**
But Daisy slept on.

Jim **rang** a bell.

He **banged** two
lids together.

Jim **stamped**.   He **sang**.

He **cried**.
But Daisy slept on.

The children tried to wake Daisy up.
They **banged**. They **clapped**.

They **tooted**.
Daisy slept on.

The farm animals tried to wake
Daisy up.

The pig **grunted**.

The sheep **baa-ed**.

The cat **meowed**. The dog **barked**.

The horse **neighed**.
The goat **bleated**.

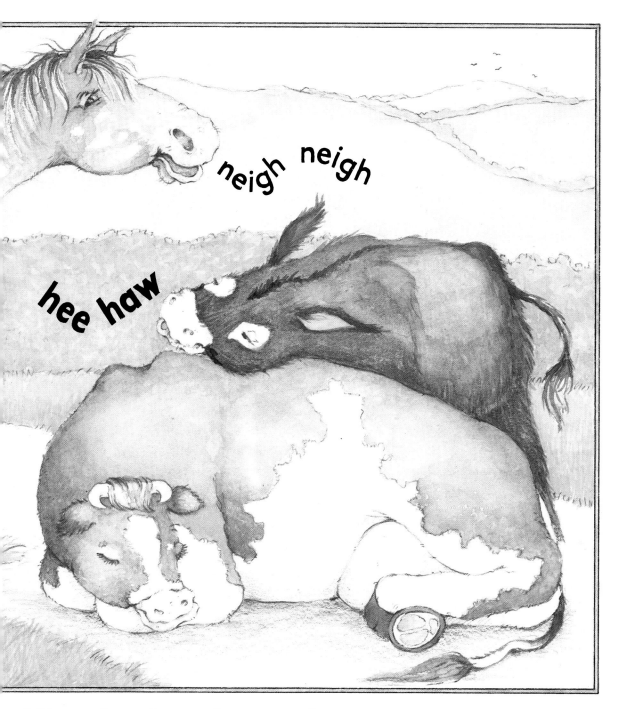

The donkey **brayed**.
Daisy slept.

The rooster **crowed**.   The duck **quacked**

The goose **hissed**.   The hen **clucked**.

The bees **buzzed**.

The mouse **squeaked**.

The cuckoo **sang**.　　The crow **cawed**.

By now there was quite a traffic jam.
Jim had one last idea.

"All together, now,
1 - 2 - 3!" called Jim.

Everyone called loudly.
The **noise** was unbelievable!

But it didn't do the trick.
Daisy slept on.

Then along came another cow.

"Moooo," she said quietly in Daisy's ear. And guess what?

Daisy woke up!
She strolled into the meadow.

And Jim and the children
went to town. Quietly.

Things To Do

1. Listen to some sounds in the kitchen:

   boiling   water running
   a timer   toast coming up
   milk pouring   garbage disposal
   cupboard door   dishwasher
   popcorn popping   steam

   Can you name these sounds
   without looking?

2. Make the sounds of these animals:

   pig   dog   bird
   cat   cow   sheep
   horse   chicken   rooster

3. Make your own musical instruments:

> Blow gently into the top of an empty soda bottle.
>
> Fill glasses with different levels of water. Tap lightly on the rims with a pencil.
>
> Stretch four or five rubber bands of different widths around a shoe box. Pluck them.
>
> Cover a comb with waxed paper. Hum on the teeth of the comb.

4. Play this game with a friend. Clap a rhythm pattern. Have your friend answer by clapping the same rhythm. Take turns.

More Books About Sounds

Bremen-Town Musicians. Plume (Doubleday)
The Ear Book. Perkins (Random House)
High Sounds, Low Sounds. Branley (Harcourt
    Brace Jovanovich)
Mama Don't Allow. Hurd (Harper Trophy)
Max the Music Maker. Stecher and Kandell
    (Lothrop, Lee & Shepard)
Noisy Book. Brown (Harper & Row)
Sounds! Lee (Gareth Stevens)

meow

bang
bang

tra-la-la

ding
dong

baa-baa

baa-baa
baa-baa

baa-baa

oink
oink

baa-baa
baa-baa

baa-baa

neigh neigh

hisssss

clomp
clomp

clap
clap

boo-hoo!

cluck
cluck

bang clash

woof!
woof!

meh-eh-eh